The Pink Ribbon Path

Prayers, Reflections and Meditations
for women with breast cancer

For all on this path,
with love and hope,
woman to woman,
heart to heart.

Mary Ussher
Pilgrim

The Pink Ribbon Path

First published in 2013 by
the columba press
55A Spruce Avenue, Stillorgan Industrial Park,
Blackrock, Co. Dublin

Cover design by sin é design
Cover illustration: Calligraphic tree with bird on top
accompanying 'To My Mother',
a poem by Thomas Moore

Origination by The Columba Press
Printed and bound by
CPI Group (UK) Ltd, Croydon, CR0 4YY

ISBN 978 1 78218 085 2

The English Standard Version is the preferred translation for Scriptural quotations within the text.

My thanks could never adequately be expressed to all those, especially my family, who are or have been guides and supporters to me on the Pink Ribbon Path.

MU

Contents

*To aid *Loving Mind–Body Awareness* and *Christian Meditation* the audio of these chapters is available to stream or download through the Columba Press website: http://www.columba.ie/index.php/pinkribbonpath.html

O Woman

O woman, clothed in the sun
with the moon at your feet
crown of twelve stars on your head
pink ribbon at your breast
queen of hope
queen of healing
queen of peace

pray for us

MU

Introduction

When a woman is diagnosed with breast cancer, life becomes a whirl of new information, it takes on a new dimension, revolving around scans, bloods, markers, infusions, and side effects, of which the most dreaded is hair loss. Too easily overlooked in all of this is the force within us with its wonderful message: we can be ill, yet whole. Inner wholeness was something I discovered and reclaimed during my treatment for breast cancer, and it has become for me a true ally, not just in my illness but in all of my life.

This book is an invitation to women with breast cancer to consider trying to re-find that wholeness, as I did, on the Pink Ribbon Path. It is a path for healing, for living, for hope, a journey which once embarked upon becomes a daily joy.

From the time I joined the cancer community in 2009 I kept a journal in which I wrote down personal reflections and transcribed prayers or words that I found inspiring. This I did during the different stages of breast cancer: on diagnosis, during treatment; after treatment; and after that, when life and living became renewed sources of profound joy. During this time, the Pink Ribbon Path slowly emerged, a spiritual path enabling rediscovery of inner strength and thus of undivided wholeness. This spiritual flourishing means meeting with awareness whatever challenges arise. Whatever the circumstances, whatever the outlook, you are not alone in your illness. The Spirit is walking with you.

Wholeness and resourcefulness encourage transcendence in relation to what is so often feared by cancer patients: recurrence of the illness. This book, I hope, will speak equally to women whose breast cancer has returned. I pray that, for all women, it may be a reminder, alongside medical treatment and care, to seek the treasure within.

The *Pink Ribbon Path* reflects the emotions I felt at each stage of the journey: the fear when out of the blue there was a diagnosis of breast cancer; the hope that medical treatment would be effective; the new and different fears and anxieties that followed treatment; then, the slow evolution of spiritual flourishing, come what may. Through these emotions I found myself growing 'downwards', towards my inner, true self. Perspectives changed.

Being on any path needs discipline, although once that path becomes a way of joyful living, time is made, willingly, for the daily journey. A transforming event for me on the Pink Ribbon Path was encountering Christian Meditation. Dom John Main OSB summarised its effect well: 'When we meditate, not only do we stand back from the individual operations of our being, but we begin to learn to find a wholly new ground to stand on. We discover a rootedness of being. The rootedness is not just in ourselves, but we discover ourselves rooted in God. Rooted in God who is Love.'

Christian Meditation is an act of love. It does not produce bells and whistles during our silence. But over time we find love growing in our heart, we become lovingly attentive to our selves in our everyday, just as we are, however tired or weak. At the same time, we reach out to others compassionately. And as we know that God has sent his Spirit to dwell in us, we become open, rooted, to his Being. This rootedness or wholeness brings greater clarity, and forgiveness of anything that may stand in the way of his Love. It facilitates a choice of responses to events rather than reactions to them. Anyone going through major illness will know how often their reactions are driven by fear.

Hazrat Inayat Khan says that the mind is the surface of the heart, the heart the depth of the mind. The Pink Ribbon Path is the path of the heart. If you have been diagnosed with breast cancer, whether for the first time or otherwise, I hope you will regard this book as a companion on successive stages of the journey, using the readings for reflection at each stage, perhaps composing and adding your own. Needless to say, you may join the Path whatever the stage of your illness: the journey inwards may begin at any time. A Loving Mind–Body Awareness, narrated by Sue Norton, who I thank, follows the four stages in the book. This stopping and becoming lovingly aware of our mind and body is integral to the journey, from the beginning. It is as much a part of the Path as the two daily meditation sessions to which we listen with the ear of the heart. Dom Laurence Freeman OSB, director of the World Community for Christian Meditation, has kindly provided meditations to listen to, and there is a wealth of other material available on the World Community for Christian Meditation website (www.wccm.org).

May Loving Awareness and Christian Meditation accompany you daily at every stage of your life.

Mary Ussher
25 August 2013

Diagnosis

Mother

How powerfully the Spirit
worked in you
dear mother
for I could not have known
anything was wrong

Yet upstairs while you prayed
I noticed an apparently
innocuous change
in my breast
and made a call

MU

But now … the hurricane has come, and you feel you are being shaken by a force that could uproot century-old trees. You feel this from without and from within. But you must remain confident, for your Faith and your Love cannot be uprooted, nor can you be blown from your way …

Contra spem in spem! – live in certain hope, against all hope. Rely on that firm rock which will save you and help you on.

You spoke about the scenes in the life of Jesus which moved you most: when he brought peace and health to those whose bodies and souls were racked with pain … You were inspired – you went on – seeing him cure leprosy, restore sight to the blind, heal the paralytic at the pool: the poor beggar forgotten by everybody. You are able to contemplate Him as He was, so profoundly human, so close at hand!
—Well! Jesus continues being the same as then.

St Josemariá Escrivá,
Extracts from Furrow

Take My Hand

I am being asked to carry
a heavy cross

Dearest Father
I am your little child

I am being asked to carry
a heavy cross

Dearest Father
Take my hand

I have never needed you so much

MU

Out of the depths I cry to you, O Lord!
O Lord, hear my voice!
Let your ears be attentive
to the voice of my pleas for mercy!

I wait for the Lord, my soul waits,
and in his word I hope;
my soul waits for the Lord
more than watchmen for the morning,
more than watchmen for the morning.

Psalm 130:1–2, 5–6

Likewise the Spirit helps us in our weakness. For we do not know what to pray for as we ought, but the Spirit himself intercedes for us with groanings too deep for words. And he who searches hearts knows what is the mind of the Spirit, because the Spirit intercedes for the saints according to the will of God. And we know that God causes all things to work together for good to those who love God, to those who are called according to this purpose.

St Paul, Romans 8: 26–8

Love

Husband, lover, partner, best friend
Never has our one-ness
been so sacramental

In sickness now
our union
Cover me with your love

MU

Thus says the Lord who made you,
who formed you from the womb and will help you:
Fear not.

Isaiah 44:2

Jesus did not come to explain away suffering or to remove it. He came to fill it with his presence.

Paul Claudel

God is our refuge and strength,
a very present help in trouble.
Therefore we will not fear though the earth gives way,
though the mountains be moved into the heart of the sea;
though its waters roar and foam,
though the mountains tremble at its swelling.

Psalm 46:1–3

Calming the Storm

I see Jesus with his disciples in the boat
beset by a gale and breaking waves.
They wake him saying, 'Master, do you not
care? We are going down.'

He orders the sea to be calm
and the wind to drop.
Then he says to them,
'Why are you so frightened?
How is it that you have no faith?'
The disciples were filled with awe.

I believe Jesus is in this boat, with me.

Lord Jesus, I trust in you.
Help me. Calm my fears.

MU

Pray, Hope and Don't Worry.

St Pio of Pietrelcina

Do not be afraid!
Open the doors to Christ.
God works in the concrete and personal affairs of each one of us.

Blessed John Paul II

Let not your hearts be troubled. Believe in God; believe also in me. … I am the way, the truth and the life.

John 14:1, 6

He did not say,
'You will not be troubled:
you will not be laboured;
you will not be afflicted.'
But he did say,
'You will not be overcome.'

Julian of Norwich

Jesus said, 'Come to me, all who labour and are heavy laden, and I will give you rest. Take my yoke upon you, and learn from me; for I am gentle and lowly in heart, and you will find rest for your souls. For my yoke is easy, and my burden is light.'

Matthew 11:28–30

Prayer

Father
thank you

for the precious gift
of my son

may he
know your love

be strong
as you are strong

endure
with courage and with faith

the news
he heard today

MU

As [Jesus] passed by, he saw a man blind from birth. And his disciples asked him, 'Rabbi, who sinned, this man or his parents, that he was born blind?' Jesus answered, 'It was not that this man sinned, or his parents, but that the works of God might be displayed in him.'
Jesus then healed his blindness.

John 9:2–3

Abide in me, and I in you. … If you abide in me, and my words abide in you, ask whatever you wish, and it will be done for you.

John 15:4, 7

This man lives in one light with God, and therefore there is not in him either suffering or the passage of time, but an unchanging eternity. From this man, truly, all wonderment has been taken away, and all things are essentially present in him. Therefore nothing new will come to him out of future events or accidents, for he dwells always anew in a now without ceasing.

Meister Eckhart Sermon 2

Child-Adult

Ease my sensitivities Lord
about people and what
may be imparted
concerning me.

At times like these
I feel my fragility
how utterly
I depend on you.

Child-Adult
may I be child alone
renewing each day
the newness of the day.

MU

When you say a situation or person is hopeless, you are slamming the door in the face of God.

Charles L. Allen

Ask and it will be given to you; seek and you will find; knock, and it will be opened to you. For everyone who asks receives, and the one who seeks finds, and to the one who knocks it will be opened. Or which one of you, if his son asks him for bread, will give him a stone? Or if he asks for a fish, will give him a serpent? If you then, who are evil, know how to give good gifts to your children, how much more will your Father who is in heaven give good things to those who ask Him! …

The gate is narrow and the way is hard that leads to life.

Matthew 7:7–11, 14

I wish you could convince yourself that God is often nearer in times of illness and weakness than when we are in a perfect state of health.

Bro. Lawrence of the Resurrection

Now

May I be aware
of you
in-dwelling
may the sacrament of
the present moment
make past past
future fiction
and break the continuum
of illness

MU

Asking in Jesus' name means entering into him, living by him, being one with him in love and faith. If he is in us by faith, in love, in grace, in his Spirit, then our petition arises from the centre of our being which is himself, and if all our petition and desire is gathered up and fused in him and his Spirit, then the Father hears us. Then our petition becomes simple and straightforward, harmonious, sober and unpretentious. Then what St Paul says in the letter to the Romans applies to us: we do not know how to pray as we ought but the Spirit himself intercedes for us praying the one prayer, 'Abba! Father!' He longs for that from which the Spirit and Jesus have proceeded: he longs for God, he asks God for God, on our behalf he asks of God. Everything is included and contained in this prayer ... [If we pray in this way] we shall see that God really answers our prayer, in one way or another.

Karl Rahner SJ

Totus Tuus [All Yours]

I know Lord
if I live
this moment
and the next
and the next
with you

I can cope

MU

O shepherd of souls,
O first of words,
Through which we all were created,
may it please you, may it please:
free us from our fear
and fragility.

Hildegard of Bingen

All things contribute to good for those who love God … assure your soul that, if it loves God, everything will be converted to good. And although you may not see the means by which this good will happen to you, be assured that it will happen … [God] has protected you up to the present moment; just remain firmly in the hands of His providence and He will help you in all situations and at those times when you find yourself unable to walk, He will carry you. What should you fear, my dearest daughter, since you belong to God who has so strongly assured us that for those who love Him all things turn into happiness. Do not think of what may happen tomorrow, because the same eternal Father who takes care of you today, will take care of you tomorrow and forever.

St Francis de Sales

What Cancer Cannot Do

It cannot cripple love,
It cannot shatter hope,
It cannot corrode faith,
It cannot eat away peace,
It cannot destroy confidence,
It cannot kill friendship,
It cannot shut out memories,
It cannot silence courage,
It cannot reduce eternal life,
It cannot quench the Spirit,
It cannot lessen the power
of the Resurrection.

Fr Harry Behan

Treatment

The Memorare

Remember, O Most Gracious Virgin Mary, that never was it known that anyone who fled to your protection, implored your help, or sought your intercession, was left unaided.

Inspired by this confidence, I come unto you, O Virgin of Virgins, my Mother, to you do I come, before you I stand, sinful and sorrowful, fearful of what is to come, O Mother of the Word incarnate, despise not my petitions, but in your mercy, hear and answer me.

Amen

Starting

Thank you Father for this day,
the tears shed
at Day Centre for the first time,
prayers in the oratory,
good bloods,
vein that carried the treatment,
welcoming consultant,
nurse who looked after me,
inventors of these infusions,
other women in the bay,
kindnesses too numerous to recall,
brother-in-law who visited,
sister who drove me home,
loving husband.

The battle has begun;
your armies are within.

MU

Sisters

They bake for you
Buy headscarves
Eyebrows, lashes
Paint with you
Pray for you
I know why
There's no
Patron saint
Of sisters

Because
Every sister
Is a saint

MU

Be still, and know that I am God.

Psalm 46:10

Let not your hearts be troubled. Believe in God; believe also in me.

John 14:1

If you ask me for anything in my name, I will do it.

John 14:14

For I will restore health to you, and your wounds I will heal, declares the Lord.

Jeremiah 30:17

We must confine ourselves to the present moment, without taking thought for the one before or the one to come.

Jean-Pierre de Caussade SJ

The Wounded Man

I think of the parable of the Good Samaritan which Jesus told in response to the question 'Who is my Neighbour?' We are told only descriptive things about the wounded man. I like to imagine that as he lay on the ground, stripped, beaten and half dead, he asked God to help him, for only the Father could. That help came after the disappointments of the priest and the Levite respectively. But the Samaritan represented God's help, which saved the wounded man. The man was not a victim, he placed his trust in God, and that trust persevered until he was rescued.

So it is for the sick. We should place our trust firmly in our Father and never falter even if he tries us by not responding immediately.

God, in the name of your Son,
May I not
speak, act or pray
like a victim

MU

Take life in instalments, this one day now. At least let this be a good day. Be always beginning. Let the past go. Now let me do whatever I have power to do. The saints were always beginning. That is how they became saints.

Worry won't mend matters.

Prayer is the greatest power on earth.

Fr John Sullivan SJ
Servant of God

This, My Everyday

Help me to accept my everyday
just as it is,
the quirky pains and aches
all over,
tenderness in hands and feet.
This, my everyday
I lay before you as it is.

Help me to love my everyday,
every moment
where I can be 'all there' with you
and 'all here'
giving myself unreservedly to this oneness.
This, my everyday
I lay before you as it is.

Thank you for this everyday,
your healing touch
in every cell,
re-bodying me,
my presence to my deepest self.
This, my everyday
I lay before you as it is.

MU

Father

Fill me with the healing power of your Spirit.
Cast out anything that should not be in me.
Mend what is broken.
Root out any unproductive cells. …

Let the warmth of your healing love pass
through my body to make new any
unhealthy areas,
so that my body will function the way you
created it to function.
And Father, restore me to full health
in body, mind and spirit
so that I may serve you
for the rest of my life.
I ask this through Christ Our Lord

Amen

Extract from anonymous Prayer for Healing

*The Port**

Thank God for the port.
I no longer need to drink three pints of water
before arriving, nor soak my hands
in warm water for ten minutes.
Today I am asked to relax and lie back
so the needle can be inserted in the port.
'We'll go on three,' says the nurse.
'Deep breath in, deep breath out, that's one;
deep breath in, deep breath out, that's two;
deep breath in, here we go – well done!
Very good blood return.'
Soon she's labelling a phial of blood and
I open my eyes and say 'thank God'
and I know verily you are the Way.

MU

*Portacath / Port catheter

Little children never realise all that their words imply, but if their father or mother were to come to the throne and inherit great riches, loving their little ones more than they love themselves, they would not hesitate to give them everything they want.

St Thérèse of Lisieux, The Story of a Soul

May I Be Healed

Ut videam, Domine.

I want to follow you along the road
like Bartimaeus, the blind beggar, shouting,
Son of David, Jesus, have pity on me.
I want you to hear me, to call me
as you did Bartimaeus.
Call him here you said
and the people called the blind man,
who, throwing off his cloak,
jumped up and went to you.
I want, too, to hear you call
so that, soul brimming, I may go to you
and hear your words,
what do you want me to do for you?

Bartimaeus, asked that question, said
Master, let me see again
for he had not always been blind.
Master, let me be well again, heal me,
make me as I was before, Rabbuni,
Son of David, Jesus, have pity on me.
Turn to me, as you did to Bartimaeus,
and say
Go, your faith has saved you.
And I will say
What do you want me, Lord, to do for you?

MU

Take comfort; before long God will heal you.

Raphael the Archangel to Tobias

No soul that has ever called upon my mercy has ever been disappointed … I am love and mercy itself. Let no one fear to draw near to me … The graces of my mercy are drawn by means of one vessel only, and that is – trust. The more a soul trusts, the more it will receive.

St Faustina Kowalska,
quoting the words spoken to her by Jesus

Commit your way to the Lord;
trust in him, and he will act.

Psalm 37:5

You Are Here

Once more I am in my bay,
needle in, bloods done,
starting the pre-meds
I introduce myself to my companions
Brian, Brenda, who's the third?
better leave her be,
it's her first day and she's in tears
her partner lingered for a while
now he's gone
I notice her long, auburn hair
hair here is rare
the book she holds
receives her tears
all round me
people are hooked up to IV lines,
some in wheelchairs, many dozing.
God is present in each one of us.

'Bidden or unbidden,
God is here.'*

MU

* Inscription on doorway of Carl Jung's house

Teach us, good Lord,
to serve thee as thou deservest;
To give, and not to count the cost;
To fight, and not to heed the wounds;
To toil, and not to seek for rest;
To labour, and not to ask for any reward
Save that of knowing that we do thy will,
Through Jesus Christ our Lord, Amen.

St Ignatius Loyola

Are not two sparrows sold for a penny? And not one of them will fall to the ground apart from your Father. But even the hairs of your head are all numbered. Fear not, therefore; you are of more value than many sparrows.

Matthew 10:29–31

Needlepark

Dear chemo, travel
in top gear,
aim with the accuracy
of an Exocet,
destroy bad cells,
avoid the good,
you know by now
how welcome you are.

Triune God,
Father, Son, and Holy Spirit.
One in Three
outnumber me today
in 'Needlepark'.

MU

Do not be afraid to tell Jesus that you love him, even though you may not feel that love. In this way you will compel him to come to your aid, and to carry you like a little child who is too weak to walk.

St Thérèse of Lisieux

Refuge

I am suffering
the pain of it clouds
your face, Father

I am not well enough
to go anywhere
I will go into my castle
and seek you

Your child is lost
fill her illness
with your presence

MU

Sacred Heart of Jesus,
I place all my trust in Thee.
Sacred Heart of Jesus,
I believe in your love for me.
Sacred Heart of Jesus,
I believe you love me now.

Fr John Sullivan SJ,
Servant of God

Do Not Be Afraid

Noli timere, dear breast.
God is on the case,
nursing and healing.

While sleeping,
He loves you.
While being treated,
He loves you.

Dear breast, dearly loved,
feel the power of the Father,
trust in him.

MU

And there was a woman who had had a discharge of blood for twelve years, and who had suffered much under many physicians, and had spent all that she had, and was no better, but rather grew worse. She had heard the reports about Jesus, and came up behind him in the crowd and touched his garment. For she said, 'If I but touch even his garments, I will be made well.'

And immediately the flow of blood dried up, and she felt in her body that she was healed of her disease.

And Jesus, perceiving in himself that power had gone out from him, immediately turned about in the crowd and said, 'Who touched my garments?'

And his disciples said to him, 'You see the crowd pressing around you; and yet you say, "Who touched me?"'

And he looked round to see who had done it. But the woman, knowing what had happened to her, came in fear and trembling, and fell down before him and told him the whole truth. And he said to her, 'Daughter, your faith has made you well; go in peace, and be healed of your disease.'

Mark 5:25–34

New Accessories

Mustn't forget the tea tree oil
or lavender cream
for hands and nails.
Mustn't forget the E45
for scalp and feet.
I see in the mirror
woolly white wisps
clinging to my crown.
Dear Lord, help me to discover
through this bitter cross
who I really am,
what I really believe.

MU

Fever

I have brought back a good message from
the land of 102 (degrees):
God exists.
… it is truth long known
that some secrets are hidden from health.

John Updike

My Guardian Dear

O Angel of God my Guardian dear
today you prompted me
to ask about my markers.
I was overjoyed to hear
since treatment began
they have reduced by fifty per cent;
fifty per cent!
You took me off to the Oratory
where we danced, and we danced,
and we hugged.
O Angel of God my Guardian dear
to whom God's love commits me here.

MU

Let nothing disturb thee,
Let nothing affright thee,
All things pass;
God changes not.
With patience everything is
accomplished.
Whoever has God
lacks nothing.
God alone suffices.

St Teresa of Avila's Bookmark
Translation by Seán Réamonn

Thoughts

In my bay
pre-meds done, chemo on the drip
I thank God for the wonder of it all
seed of the yew nourished by
soil inhabited by earthworms
sapling sprouting to
sun and rain
sheltering insects in
maturing tree
magnificent creation's indwelling powers
of healing, rebalancing, rebodying
I thank God for the one who drew out
these powers, was she – or he – someone
fired 'to make a difference'
to extract from the ancient tree
its secrets
stewarding God's manifold gifts
so that a woman such as I might be healed

MU

After Treatment

Hail, Holy Queen

Hail, Holy Queen, Mother of mercy!
Hail, our life, our sweetness and our hope!
To thee do we cry, poor banished
children of Eve: to thee do we send
up our sighs, mourning and weeping
in this valley of tears.
Turn then, most gracious advocate,
thine eyes of mercy toward us; and
after this our exile, show unto us the
blessed fruit of thy womb, Jesus.

O clement, O loving, O sweet Virgin Mary!

Amen

I would like the Angels of Heaven
to be among us.
I would like an abundance of peace.
I would like full vessels of charity.
I would like rich treasures of mercy.
I would like cheerfulness to preside over all.
I would like Jesus to be present.
I would like the three Marys of illustrious
renown to be with us.
I would like the friends of Heaven to be
gathered around us from all parts.
I would like myself to be a rentpayer to the
Lord; that I should suffer distress and that
He would bestow a good blessing upon me.

Brigid of Ireland

Beginning Again

Lord God, dearest Father
take away all fears
from now on
let me be all here
return to my place and
begin again
'to be
what I already am'.*

MU

* Thomas Merton OCSO

Do not be anxious about your life, what you will eat or what you will drink, nor about your body, what you will put on. Is not life more than food, and the body more than clothing? Look at the birds of the air; they neither sow nor reap nor gather into barns and yet your heavenly Father feeds them. Are you not of more value than they? And which of you by being anxious can add a single hour to his span of life? … Therefore do not be anxious, saying, 'What shall we eat?' or 'What shall we drink?' or 'What shall we wear?'

Matthew 6:25–7, 31

We are obliged to plan for the future and take thought of tomorrow. But we should do it without worrying, without the care that gnaws at the heart but doesn't solve anything – and often prevents us from putting our hearts into what we have to do here and now. Hearts anxious about tomorrow can't be open to the grace of the present moment.

Fr Jacques Philippe

My Self

I suffer when my
would-be nothingness
advocates revisions
challenging what I really believe
illness unhinges
pro tempore obliterates
power and position
the artificial self
forgive me Father
when I find it hard

The trial of my cancer has taught me
I am a child of dust

MU

Sufficient unto the day. The things that have to be done must be done, and for the rest we must not allow ourselves to become infested with thousands of petty fears and worries, so many motions of no confidence in God. Everything will turn out all right.

Etty Hillesum

Keep yourself at peace and in complete repose, never become upset and never trouble yourself about anything, forget the past, live as though the future does not exist, live for Jesus in every moment that you are living, or, better, live as though you have no life in yourself, but allow Jesus to live in you at His leisure.

St Francois-Marie-Jacob Libermann

Back to Work

This week I could compare
work, the prose of everyday life
with work, the carrying of the Cross.
I found turning that prose
into heroic verse very different from
turning those thorns into roses.
God, grant me your peace.

MU

With acknowledgment to St J. Escrivá

Peace is the simplicity of spirit, the serenity of conscience, the tranquillity of the soul and the bond of love.

St Pio of Pietrelcina

Remain at peace, my daughter. Remove from your imagination whatever may upset you and say frequently to Our Lord, 'O God, you are my God and I will trust in you; you will help me and you will be my refuge and there is nothing I will fear, because not only are you with me, but, also, you are in me and I in you.' What does a child in the arms of such a Father have to fear? Be as a little child, my dearest daughter. As you know children don't concern themselves with many matters; they have others who think for them. They are strong enough if they remain with their father. Therefore, act accordingly, my daughter, and you will be at peace.

St Francis de Sales

Not My Will

Not my will
but Yours be done.
Not this child's
but Yours, Abba.
With outstretched arms
receive me
and give me
your peace.

MU

I had no guide, no light,
Save that which burned within my heart,
And yet this light did guide my way,
More surely than the noonday sun
Unto the place where waited One
Who knew me well.

St John of the Cross, Canticle of the Soul

I have reached the stage now where I can afford to look back; in the crucible of trials from within and without, my soul has been refined, and I can raise my head like a flower after a storm and see how the words of the Psalm have been fulfilled in my case: 'The Lord is my shepherd and I shall want nothing. He hath made me to lie in pastures green and pleasant; He hath led me gently beside the waters. He hath led my soul without fatigue … Yea, though I should go down into the valley of the shadow of death, I will fear no evil, for Thou, O Lord, art with me.'

St Thérèse of Lisieux

Peace v. Anxiety

Peace I seek
roots ever deepening
nourished by
the grace of God

Anxiety I spurn
plant of darkness
unbidden, sour
unwelcome

MU

Cast all your anxiety on him, because he cares for you.

1 Peter 5:7

And we know that for those who love God all things work together for good.

Romans 8:28

The value of persistent prayer is not that God will hear us, but that we will finally hear God.

William J. McGill

When one door of happiness closes, another one opens, but we look so long at the closed door that we do not see the one which has been opened for us.

Helen Keller

Deal bountifully with your servant,
 that I may live and keep your word.

Psalm 119:17

Vultum tuum, Domine, requiram.
Your Face, O Lord, do I seek.

Psalm 27:8

Resolutions

I pray that
old habits stay away
resolutions
made during
illness endure

may the different contour
and play of each day
become and remain
my jewels

MU

Every morning, when we wake up, we
have twenty-four brand new hours to live.
What a precious gift!
We have the capacity to live in a way that
these twenty-four hours will bring peace,
joy, and happiness to ourselves and others.

Peace is present right here and now, in
ourselves and in everything we do and
see. …

We can smile, breathe, walk, and eat our
meals in a way that allows us to be in touch
with the abundance of happiness that is
available.

Thich Nhat Hanh

May They Be

Hello scanner, my old friend
I've come to talk with you again.
Same old vision softly creeping
When awake or when I am sleeping.
And the vision that was planted
In my brain still remains –
Stable scans: survival.

MU

With acknowledgement to Simon and Garfunkel,
The Sound of Silence

I lift up my eyes to the hills.
From where does my help come?
My help comes from the Lord,
who made heaven and earth.

He will not let your foot be moved;
he who keeps you will not slumber.
Behold, he who keeps Israel
will neither slumber nor sleep.

The Lord is your keeper;
the Lord is your shade on your right hand.
The sun shall not strike you by day,
nor the moon by night.

The Lord will keep you from all evil;
he will keep your life.
The Lord will keep
your going out and your coming in
from this time forth and for evermore.

Psalm 121

Protecting the Present

I must not allow my present
to be burdened by the weight
of the past few years
but worse would be
to allow the future's imagined weight
to burden my present.
Mary, help me to remain
at peace, to say always
to your Son
In you I trust

MU

I will extol you, O Lord, for you have
drawn me up
and have not let my foes rejoice over me.
O Lord my God, I cried to you for help,
and you have healed me. ...

You have turned for me my mourning into
dancing;
O Lord my God, I will give thanks to
you for ever.

Psalm 30

And After That

The Canticle of Mary

My soul magnifies the Lord,
And my spirit rejoices in God my Saviour;
Because he has regarded the lowliness of
his handmaid;
For behold, henceforth all generations shall
call me blessed; because he who is mighty
has done great things for me,
and holy is his name;
And his mercy is from generation to
generation on those who fear him.
He has shown might with his arm,
he has scattered the proud in the conceit of
their heart.
He has put down the mighty from their
thrones, and has exalted the lowly.
He has filled the hungry with good things,
and the rich he has sent away empty.
He has given help to Israel, his servant,
mindful of his mercy:
Even as he spoke to our fathers, to
Abraham and to his posterity forever.

Rise up, my soul, rise up, shake off the dust, lift yourself up, and enter before the gaze of the Lord, your God, to confess before him all the mercy and compassion that he has shown to you.

Blessed are you, Adonai,
in the firmament of heaven.
Let all the marrow and
virtue of my spirit bless you.
Let all the substance
of my soul and body bless you.
Let all that is within me glorify you.

St Gertrude the Great of Helfta

Hearing the Flowers

Slow down
Don't move too fast
Want to make
Each moment last

Want to hear
The flowers grow
Feel their rhythm
In my soul

MU

With acknowledgement to Simon & Garfunkel,
The 59th Street Bridge Song

One time our good Lord said:
All things shall be well;
And another time he said:
Thou shalt see thyself that all manner *[of] things shall be well.*

Julian of Norwich

The Lord is my light and my salvation;
whom shall I fear?
The Lord is the stronghold of my life;
of whom shall I be afraid?

Psalm 27:1

For nothing will be impossible with God.

Luke 1:37

The Tandem Bike Ride

At first, I saw God as my observer, my judge, keeping track of things I did to know whether I merited heaven or hell. God was 'out there' – sort of like a president: I recognised his picture, but I did not know him.

Later on, when I met Jesus, life became a bike ride. It was a tandem bike, and Jesus was in the back helping me pedal. I don't know at what point he suggested we change places, but life has not been the same since then.

When I had the control, I knew the way. It was rather boring, but predictable. It was the shortest distance between two points. When Jesus led we took delightful longcuts – up mountains and through rocky places at breakneck speeds. It was all I could do to hang on! Even though it looked like madness, he said, 'Pedal!'

I worried and was anxious and asked, 'Where are you taking me?' He laughed, but didn't answer.

I forgot my boring life and entered into the adventure. And when I would say 'I'm scared' he'd lean back and touch my hand. He took me to people who gave me gifts of healing, acceptance, joy, and peace for our journey. He said, 'Share the gifts.' So I did – to the people we met. And I found that in giving I received, and our burden was light.

I did not trust him at first to control my life. I thought he'd wreck it. But he knows how to make bikes bend and take sharp corners, jump to clear high rocks, fly to shorten scary passages.

I am learning to be quiet and pedal in the strangest places. I'm beginning to enjoy the view and the cool breeze on my face. And when I'm sure I just can't do anymore, he just smiles and says, 'Pedal!'

Author Unknown

Inhaling the Spirit

Someone said about prayer:
'It's exhaling the spirit of man
And inhaling the spirit of God.'

I exhale the past
and inhale the present
the wondrous, life-giving present.

MU

My Lord God, I have no idea where I am going.

I do not see the road ahead of me. I cannot know for certain where it will end.

Nor do I really know myself, and the fact that I think I am following your will does not mean that I am actually doing so.

But I believe that the desire to please you does in fact please you, and I hope I have that desire in all that I am doing.

And I know that if I do this, You will lead me by the right road, though I may know nothing about it.

Therefore I will trust you always though I may seem to be lost in the shadow of death.

I will not fear, for you are ever with me, and you will never leave me to face my struggle alone.

Thomas Merton OCSO

The Seasons

For most everything there is a season
A time to be told about illness
A time to take stock
A time for treatment
A time to recover
A time for re-centring
A time to glimpse hope
A time to frame plans

MU

I call to you, O God:
Give me what I need to live!
You have good plans for me;
I may see you and know you.

Hildegard of Bingen

For surely I know the plans I have for you, says the Lord, plans for your welfare and not for harm, to give you a future with hope. Then when you call upon me and come and pray to me, I will hear you.

Jeremiah 29:11–12 (NRSV)

Fear not, for I am with you; be not dismayed, for I am your God; I will strengthen you, I will help you, I will uphold you with my rightious right hand.

Isaiah 41:10

I

B
R
E
A
T
H
E

N O W N O T I

Y
O
U

B
R
E
A
T
H
E

M
E

MU

Dulcis hospes animae meae

Sweet guest of my soul
Spirit within
He in me and
I in him
For ever resting
in my Friend

MU

Summa cum laude

If breast cancer returns
I'll be a postgraduate
at a school I call
the school of blessings
I was nervous
when matriculating
but Mary led me to her Son

His love made me thrive
enlarged my heart
to the whole universe
when I graduated
neither pain nor death
held me in thrall

whoever would have thought
cancer could be God's megaphone

MU

Make a joyful noise to the Lord,
all the earth!
Serve the Lord with gladness!
Come into his presence with singing!

Know that the Lord, he is God!
It is he that made us, and we are his;
we are his people, and the sheep of his
pasture.

Enter his gates with thanksgiving,
and his courts with praise!
Give thanks to him; bless his name!

For the Lord is good;
his steadfast love endures for ever,
and his faithfulness for all generations.

Psalm 100

Holding Hands

Take my hand, hold it
No need to explain why you
Asked to meet, I knew by the
Quiver in your voice
Now we're sipping coffee
You tell me
That 'worrisome' tumour is malignant
You have breast cancer

Leave your hand in mine
Your colleagues never knew, you say,
Those meetings 'out of the office'
Were for cat scans, MRIs,
Lumbar punctures, mammograms,
Ultrasounds, bloods, you led
A double life until you got the news
You have breast cancer

Put both hands in mine
I can believe how devastated
Your loved ones are
Your partner's numb and wordless
Your parents and your children
Speak through tears
Your sisters and your brothers whisper
You have breast cancer

Feel the power in my hands
Know with certainty
That God is present, longing
For you to seek him
He is with you already
On your Pink Ribbon Path
Closer than ever before because
You have breast cancer

MU

I see His Blood upon the Rose

I see his blood upon the rose
And in the stars the glory of his eyes,
His body gleams amid eternal snows,
His tears fall from the skies.

I see his face in every flower;
The thunder and the singing of the birds
Are but his voice – and carven by his
power
Rocks are his written words.

All pathways by his feet are worn,
His strong heart stirs the ever-beating sea.
His crown of thorns is twined with every
thorn,
His cross is every tree.

Joseph Mary Plunkett

Thanksgiving

What can I render to the Lord
For all that he has
Rendered unto me.

For the continuing gift of life
For sparing and transforming it
I thank you.

For each new sunrise
And birdsong, your liturgy,
I thank you.

For sleeping to the gift of rest
And rising to the gift of life
I thank you.

For winter-flowering cherry blossom,
My father's rose, and lavender
I thank you.

For every cell and particle
Restored to your healing
I thank you.

For hair and nails re-grown
And new peace in my deepest core
I thank you.

For love of husband, child, mother
Siblings, spouses
I thank you.

For support of pink sisters
And tireless friends along the way
I thank you.

For nurses, doctors, their infusions
Cheery women who brought the tea
I thank you.

For every tear in near despair
The love in your Cross
I thank you.

For help in the battle
Between faith and fear
I thank you.

For having heard and answered me
Especially when I could not pray
I thank you.

For passage to a new life
Beyond all imagining
I thank you.

For new lens to discern
'success' and 'worry'
I thank you.

For Your Spirit's awesome presence
O uncreated One
I thank you.

For the music of your silence
Sweetest surrender
I thank you.
And I pray that all women
on the Pink Ribbon Path
may find and love you, Lord.
That, by your grace,
if I am again afflicted
with this disease
I may remain on the Path.
That through Mary my prayers may be
an instrument of hope;
and that one day, O God of life,
breast cancer will be overcome.

MU

The Pink Ribbon Path

The Pink Ribbon Path
Is the path of the heart
Where the cry of the heart
Is heard

I will stay on this path
Walk straight in its curves
I will not be afraid
I will not be perturbed

The Pink Ribbon Path
Is the path of the heart
Where the ear of the heart
Hears You

MU

Loving Mind–Body Awareness AND *Christian Meditation*

Opening Prayer

Glory be to the Father
And to the Son
And to the Holy Spirit

O God, come to our aid.
O Lord, make haste to help us.
Holy Spirit, release in us
your healing power.
Flood our heart-room with
your loving presence,
and radiate your love
to every part of our mind and body.

Loving Mind–Body Awareness

What follows is the text of the audio exercise read by Sue Norton. Sue Norton is lecturer of English in the Dublin Institute of Technology and a freelance essayist. She is American and has lived in Ireland for many years. Sue has gifted her honorarium for this recording to Smilow Cancer Hospital (http://yalecancercenter.org/gifts/index.aspx).

Give your full body weight to where you are resting. There's nowhere to go, nothing you have to do at this time. This is a time for complete rest, unconditional love and healing. You are about to do a Loving Mind–Body Awareness. A prayer for healing. Sending loving care to every part of you, every cell and particle.

Become aware of your mind.
In this moment
lovingly let go.
Allow all tension
to fall away, seep away,
slowly.
Allow your mind
to be completely
at ease, in peace, restful.

Give thanks to your mind
for its capacity to find
a life of beauty and truth.
Send loving-kindness
to its infinite potential
for healing.

Become aware of the
deep centre of your self,
the core of your being,

from which loving kindness
flows to every part of you,
to others and
to creation.

Become aware of
your heart of love.

The love
you give and receive;
the love you have
for your self;
gentle, kind self-acceptance,
deep friendship with
every aspect of your self.

Now, become aware of your body,
resting where it is,
breathing in and
breathing out,
letting go all tension.

Lovingly turn your attention to your feet;
feel the full weight of both feet
where you are resting
from your heels to your toes.
Be aware of your ankles,
of both your legs,
coming up to your knees,
continuing on past your knees,
up the back of your thighs,

aware of both your legs easing and sinking
where you are resting.
And now coming to the base of the spine,
aware that it is heavy where it is resting.

Lovingly become aware
of your kidneys, your liver.
Let your love dwell
in the whole of your abdomen.
Continue this loving awareness
up your spine,
slowly up your spine,
through each vertebra,
bit by bit,
slowly, slowly, to the top of the spine;
coming deep down in between the
shoulders,
easing and releasing the shoulders.

Send loving kindness to your breathing.
Breathing in and breathing out.
Breathing in and breathing out.
Watch the rise and fall of the breath.
The loving breath of life
as it comes in … and flows out.
Really letting it flow out
in your very own timing.
As it comes in, really letting it flow out.
As it comes in, really letting it flow out.

And now allow the breathing to find its
own rhythm again
in the way that it wants to.

Lovingly become aware of your breasts;
your right;
your left.

Become aware of your neck
and the whole of your head,
letting the corners of your eyes really drop,
the corners of your mouth and of your jaw
really drop,
allowing your whole face to soften.
Become aware of your shoulders,
your forearms, your wrists
out to the tips of your fingers,
aware of where they are resting.

Breathing in, aware of the whole body.
Breathing out, aware of the whole body.
Breathing in, calming the whole body.
Breathing out, calming the whole body.

You are ready to take up a position of
complete attention to your right arm.

Your right arm is heavy and warm;
heavy and warm.
Your left arm is heavy and warm;
heavy and warm.

Your arms are heavy and warm.
Your right leg is heavy and warm;
heavy and warm.
Your left leg is heavy and warm;
heavy and warm.
Your arms and legs are heavy and warm.

Now, gently draw a deep breath;
starting in your belly,
moving up your abdomen,
to the base of your lungs,
your upper rib cage,
your shoulders, and your neck.
Gently exhale that deep breath.
It breathes you.
Thank the Spirit for the breath of your life.

Your solar plexus is warm.

Your neck and shoulders are heavy.

Your forehead is cool and clear;
cool and clear.

Now, invite God's infinite power
to enter every pore of your body
and your mind;
slowly, slowly
suffusing every cell and particle.

Ask the Father to direct his power
to where your body needs restoring.

Feel his power going
deeper, deeper, deeper,
to that part of your body
and to your mind.

Ask the Father to bless your treatment
and to restore you
lovingly
in this present moment
and the next, and the next.

Rest peacefully in the Lord.
Breathing in;
breathing out.

When you have finished your Loving Mind–Body Awareness, take some time to raise your arms over your head, and as you do so take a deep breath in, then lower your arms slowly back to your sides, breathing out as you do so. Do this as many times as you wish. Feel revitalised in your mind and body.

Christian Meditation

On the Pink Ribbon Path try to meditate every morning and evening for at least twenty minutes and ideally for thirty.

Christian Meditation

On the Pink Ribbon Path,
in Christian Meditation,
we stand before the Lord,
watching and waiting.

In this moment and the next
we are in the presence of God.
He breathes us, dwells within,
he does not wish us to be afflicted.

Relaxed but alert,
leave everything to him.

MU

Mindfulness

Christian Meditation is sometimes called Christian Mindfulness.

Mindfulness emphasises the presence of our total selves in the moment. Actually true recollection demands this too, but the full presence is too easily forgotten. …
[It demands] the awareness of one's self, the action, and the God who is there.

Presence to the moment … means being 'all there'. … True presence is steady, non-discursive attention, which at the same time is relaxed and self-possessed.

[In illness we are closer*] to reality and therefore to God. … Listen to these words of Karl Rahner, who puts them in the mouth of Christ: 'I am the blind alleys of all your paths, for when you no longer know how to go any further, then you have reached me.'

Ernest E. Larkin O. Carm
Extracts from article 'Christian Mindfulness'

*My insertion: *MCU*

In religious terms, people often talk about loving God, loving your neighbour and loving yourself. But I think only a little experience with meditating will show you that the true order is the other way round. You must first learn to be yourself and to love yourself. And secondly you must allow your neighbour to be themselves, and learn to love them. And it is then, and only then, that it makes any sense to talk about God.

Maranatha means 'come Lord' ... The essence of the mantra ... is that it brings you to silence. It is not a magic word. It is not a word that has any esoteric properties to it or anything like that. It is simply a word that is sacred in our tradition. Maranatha is possibly the oldest Christian prayer there is after the 'Our Father'. It is a word that brings us to great peacefulness, to rest and calm.

Fr John Main OSB
Extracts from The Way of Unknowing

Ma–ra–na–tha

Put equal emphasis on each syllable,
perhaps saying the mantra
as your breath rises.
Try to think the mantra, not say it.
Hear it.
Hear yourself saying it;
like a hum in the background
or a sound from far down a hill.
Every now and then you will be
distracted
just return to the mantra.

Ma–ra–na–tha

Getting Started

Choose somewhere quiet.
Sit, if you can, or lie down.
Close your eyes.
Relax your mouth, teeth and jaw.
Relax your body.
Become aware of the present moment;
its sounds, smells, touch.
Breathe gently and naturally.

Recollect that God dwells within you.

God is here;
you are home.

The following
written and
Freeman
permission
poems, Breathing
Christian
templative
hundred
Like
First
Centuries
describe
Spiritual
Do We Meditate
question
it's easier
fully alive.
Following this
the Christian life

Meditations

by Dom Laurence Freeman OSB

The following pages, also on audio, are written and narrated by Dom Laurence Freeman OSB and included with his kind permission. Dom Laurence is a Benedictine monk, Director of the World Community for Christian Meditation, a contemporary, contemplative community, now in more than a hundred countries. He is author of many articles and books including *The Selfless Self, Jesus: The Teacher Within* and *First Sight: The Experience of Faith*.

First are two pieces on meditation from the CD entitled *Being Present*. 'A Creative Work' describes meditation as a creative act, a spiritual path, 'a pearl of great price'. 'Why Do We Meditate?' answers this important question; if we understand why we meditate it's easier to keep going, and thus to become fully alive.

Following this are four meditations from the CD entitled *Letting Go*. Listen to each one before entering into silence. The first, simply called 'Meditation', describes meditation as a way of unlearning, a way of unknowing, bringing peace, 'refreshingly simple'. 'The Narrow Path' is particularly apt for those on the Pink Ribbon Path, 'better a narrow path than being lost in a trackless wasteland'. Meditation is the simplification of ourselves, the path that leads to life. 'The Sower' ponders the words of a fifth-century master of the spiritual path, Diadochos of Photiki, telling us that meditation is natural and necessary for our human development, the ultimate meaning of which is union with God. 'The discipline revolutionizes our life.' Sharing the same prefix with 'medicine', meditation is medicine for the soul. The fourth meditation, 'Friendship', shows how meditation helps us to become better friends with ourselves. Gradually we bring those hurt parts of ourselves 'under the influence of the warm, light radiation of the love that is being released in the depth of our being'.

For further information on the World Community for Christian Meditation see www.wccm.org & www.wccmmeditatio.org.

A Creative Work

All creative acts begin with a moment of stillness when we poise ourselves and we get balanced, we get ready and we give our attention to whatever it is we're going to do, like a runner ready to start a race or a singer about to perform. So it's the same now with meditation. Meditation is a creative work, for most of us it's the creative part of the day but sometimes, as with anything we do every day, we can get lazy about it or we can take it for granted. So just take a moment now to remember what a gift it is to have found this creative work, this spiritual path and what a pearl of great price meditation is.

Every time we meditate we are renewing the path. It's always the same, but it's always fresh. The mantra is like an old friend but one that always opens some new door or deepens an old wisdom. Every time we sit to meditate it's like coming home after a long journey and home is home but it's always welcoming.

The way to renew this commitment is to remember the total simplicity of what we're doing and to remember how much this simple work changes our life and our whole way of being.

So sit simply, be comfortable but alert. Take a moment to just be aware of your posture, sit with your back straight. And then take a moment to be conscious of your breath. As you breathe in you are receiving the gift of life and because it's a gift you can't possess it, you can't hold it indefinitely so you let it go naturally at the right moment when it's comfortable. And it's in this receiving and returning that the mystery of life is revealed.

Come back to yourself, into your own mind and body; you're not playing any roles; and take a moment to stop thinking of what you've done or what you haven't done today or what you're going to do and simply be who you are at this precise moment.

Close your eyes gently and let the muscles of your face, your neck, your shoulders all relax. Now turn your attention to the mantra and listen to it with generous attention. Clearly. Don't fight any distracting thoughts that come, just let them dissolve like smoke or spray and say the mantra simply. 'Unless you become like a little child you cannot enter the Kingdom of Heaven.'

And to say the mantra simply means simply that. Say it without thinking of how you're saying it or calculating what you will get out of it. Even if you become aware of being, so it seems, without thought that is itself a thought so keep returning to the mantra but with an ever deeper gentleness and precision. Meditating is like a child becoming aware of the world around it and within it for the first time, simply enjoying this creative discovery of reality. It's in listening to the mantra that silence deepens and this silence, wakeful, calm, clear, unselfconscious silence full of love is creating spirit.

Why Do We Meditate?

We need to keep asking that question because if we can understand why we meditate it's easier to keep going. Sometimes it's difficult to explain to other people if they ask you why you meditate until you know what you're doing as you meditate.

In the Gospel, Jesus describes the Kingdom of Heaven as like a woman who lost a coin and turned her house upside down trying to find it and when she found it she called in her neighbours and they had great rejoicing. In a sense meditation is like that. We're finding something that we have lost or think that we've lost. And just as when you are looking high and low for something that you've misplaced you are not quite sure where you put it, you're not even sure if it's still there, you have to keep looking for it in faith. Meditation is also a seeking in faith.

And what keeps us going is the faith that whoever seeks also finds. The faith that we meditate with, therefore, is the same faith that keeps us living hopefully and meaningfully. The faith of meditation is the conviction that life is ultimately worthwhile.

Jesus also describes the spiritual quest as losing something; losing our very self-consciousness, letting the ego-self drop away and die. Losing our life so that we can find it. Finding and losing; losing and finding. This is what we're doing when we meditate. They're both valid ways of understanding the process of understanding, the dynamic of meditation. Becoming fully alive involves finding and losing, two sides of the same coin. On some occasions we may see more of one side than the other but the commitment to the daily practice remains equal and steady, ultimately it's about perseverance.

We are really meditating in faith, this is the perseverance that we practise in the morning and in the evening every day. In the morning it may seem like finding, in the afternoon or the evening it may seem like losing. It's all the same. We're not meditating just for what we get out of it in the short term, for egotistical reasons. What the practice itself teaches us is that the losing and the finding become equally valuable, interchangeable and when we grasp that then we can really understand why we meditate. To be fully alive, to enter into the heart of the mystery of life and it's then that we really begin to discover that liberty of spirit that the daily discipline of meditation reveals.

Meditation

Whoever meditates sincerely is already a disciple, a learner, a disciple of life. But to learn at this depth of our being is not like learning facts or skills. We aren't adding to our store of knowledge or abilities. Meditation is a way of unlearning, a way of unknowing.

Lau Tzu said that learning consists of adding to your stock day by day. He said the practice of Tao consists of subtracting day by day, subtracting and yet again subtracting until one has reached inactivity.

This is ancient wisdom for modern people. I think something in us responds gratefully to this wisdom when we hear these words. What a relief when we sit to meditate to know that we don't have to do anything or gain anything, achieve anything, go anywhere, please anyone. There is no success, no failure. The true peace of meditation arises from this total freedom from inner or outer compulsion. It is refreshingly simple. In fact, it is intoxicatingly simple.

Now all this could sound very selfish; doing nothing, trying for nothing – isn't that just vegetating? But simple isn't easy. Meditation is work. It is the most beautiful and the most creative and purely loving work of the human mind and heart. We're not learning new things but we are, as Lao Tzu said, subtracting, unlearning. We're unlearning the conditioned responses of the mind to succeed, to be happy, to run from pain, to seek pleasure. We're chipping away little by little at the old ego. Leaving self behind, as Jesus said; this is what we're doing so that we can enter upon the spacious kingdom of the true self, the reign of God.

So what is the goal of this steady, silent, daily subtraction? Becoming smaller in the ego means expanding beyond all the boundaries of desire and fear that constrict us and control us. The goal, according to Lao Tzu, is inactivity. What the psalmist calls stillness. The stillness in which the divine consciousness manifests itself to us in the perfume of its all-pervasive love.

Remember this deep wisdom of the ages each time you prepare for your meditation, day by day, morning and evening. Don't evaluate or analyse your meditation and ignore the ego's desire for success and its fear of failure. Meditating alone will teach you some aspects of this through the experience of solitude. Meditating with others will teach you other aspects of it through the experience of community. But either alone or with others, you are the same person. The subtracting is the same, the faithful work of the mantra is the same. This is not the dull sameness that some people fear that it is, it is the deep stability and calm, the stillness and non-doing out of which the vast, peaceful explosion of God's beautiful creation happens.

So remember the simplicity of the teaching and practise the teaching simply and consistently. To meditate, sit down, sit with your back straight, sit still, relaxed but alert.

Close your eyes lightly and then silently, interiorly begin to say your word, your mantra. The word I would recommend is the word 'Maranatha'. If you choose that word say it as four syllables 'Ma–Ra–Na–Tha'. Maranatha. And as you say the word listen to it with attention, simply and faithfully. Let go of your thoughts, fears, desires, plans and memories. Don't fight them, don't try and repress them but just let them go and you'll let them go by faithfully returning to the mantra.

The Narrow Path

If only meditation were as easy as it is simple. The great masters of wisdom and compassion in all traditions have understood that the path is long and narrow. Jesus said, 'Enter by the narrow gate, wide is the gate and broad the road that leads to destruction and many enter that way. But narrow is the gate and constricted the path that leads to life and those who find it are few.' But better a narrow path than being lost in a trackless wasteland. The narrowness is really only the focussing of our attention. The destruction that Jesus speaks of for those who wander the broad roads of life is distraction, getting lost. It's that terrible state where you can't pay attention to anything because you lack inner peace, you lack poise and stillness and therefore you can never be with anyone, communicate with anyone, love anyone and you don't even know who you are.

The daily subtraction of Lao Tzu is the narrow path of Jesus but whatever we call it, it is the simplification of ourselves, coming to a single pointedness, a deep centre of personal integration and harmony. And that's why this path leads to life. The narrower the path the more focussed we are, then the more intense our life will be, the more alive we will be. The smaller the gate that we pass through as we pay attention then the vaster the spaces that we will learn to glide through.

We experience this narrowness in meditation in two ways; the discipline – and don't forget the word 'discipline' means learning – the discipline of meditation twice a day, regardless of what you may feel like or even how busy you are; and also the discipline of saying the mantra faithfully, returning to it lovingly throughout the whole period of the meditation, the twenty or thirty minutes that you give to meditation each morning and each evening. And remember not to judge your meditation as good or bad, successful or a failure. Most of us feel that if we have had a very distracted meditation, scattered and all over the place then we've wasted our time. Maybe there's sadness or resentment or even anger at ourselves that we blew it, that we missed the opportunity but watch out for these feelings and thoughts and when they come send them packing without delay.

Some thoughts, true spiritual insights, are like pilgrims. They arrive at our door and ask to be welcomed. Let these in at the appropriate time and receive what they give you as you entertain them. But other thoughts are robbers in disguise; if you let them get a foot in the door they will rob you of your peace and muddy your carpets. The polite visitor wipes his feet when he enters. So with these kinds of negative self-rejecting thoughts: 'I'm no good at meditation.' 'I've failed.' Wipe the floor with any thoughts that make you evaluate or analyse your spiritual journey.

You don't have to judge your spiritual journey because meditation is pure openness to unconditional love. Success or failure doesn't matter, you are loved the same. Knowing this, knowing that you are loved at the deep core of your being unconditionally and that that love is the very source of your being, knowing this is what faith means. Really knowing it is what enlightenment, wisdom, means. All that matters, St Paul said, is 'faith active in love'. And this is the mantra, faith active in love. That's a very good description of meditation. Every time you sit to meditate, every time you say your mantra with attention you are taking a step of faith and you are also deepening your capacity for love on a beautiful narrow path that leads to life.

The Sower

Words are amazing things. We can express something in words that long outlives us. Shakespeare knew this when he wrote his sonnets expressing his love and the authors of the world's sacred scriptures must have known that the words they were inspired to write would live on, inspiring others long after they, the authors, were forgotten.

Today in our media-saturated world we are bombarded by words and images. They make meditation a daily challenge and a daily necessity. The silence is more difficult but more urgently needed. Most of the these words are meaningless or malicious, the empty chatter of chat shows or the manipulation of the advertisers and persuaders and so it's all the more important that we develop a taste for the discipline of silence, that we fast from words and images and thoughts at regular times. The morning and evening meditation times offer us this precious opportunity. If we understand what we are doing we must know that these are the most valuable times of our day.

Amid all the deluge of overheated, meaningless chatter and malicious talk there are some wise, cool, enlightening words of wisdom. They flow like pure streams unaffected by the pollution around them and in fact they purify what has been polluted. These are the words of the masters of the spiritual path, simple, humble and other-centred.

At times we stumble across these masters or we seem to stumble across them, perhaps they have actually come in search of us, and maybe these words of Diadochos of Photiki, a fifth-century Christian from Greece, will be this for you as they are for me. Listen to his words:

> Only God is good. But with God's help we can become good through careful attention to our way of life. We transform

> ourselves into what we are not when we direct ourselves to true delight, uniting ourselves to God in as much as our energised power desires this.

These words point to our experience of meditation day by day. Meditation is natural and necessary for our human development and this ultimate meaning of human development is union with God. Diadochos sees simply here that this work is not just passive it is also our own responsibility; we are in a sense co-creators of ourselves with God. We can't do it just by ourselves, obviously, but God can't do it without us either. The mystery of life, of all being is the oneness of creation and creator, of source and goal. The fall of Adam was losing sight of this. The resurrection of Christ is the recovery of this vision of oneness. But it's not esoteric or abstract. As Diadochos says we need to pay careful attention to our way of life. Any sincere meditator knows that the discipline revolutionises your life. It is indeed a silent revolution but it affects the material, the psychological and the spiritual aspects of your lifestyle. The key word here is *careful* attention. That doesn't mean self-fixation, a constant self-conscious analysing of ourselves, but it means a mindful awareness of how we are spending our money, our time, our emotional and sexual energy.

The words 'meditation' and 'medicine' are united by the Greek prefix 'med', which has the sense of careful, attentive, concern. Meditation is medicine for the soul. It allows us to pay that careful attention to our life that makes us good people, good with the goodness that is God. What this means really is that we pay attention to our true selves and so we learn to be who we truly are. Meditation is about being, not doing or trying to make anything happen and yet when we do get to that simple, still, non-active being we are transformed. Diadochos said that we are transformed into what we are not, that is true but he could equally well have said we are transformed into what we are. This transformation is accomplished not by willpower, by intense effort or egotistical energy. It happens when we direct our attention to true delight. That's a wonderful insight and a very important insight for us today. And that makes the spiritual life and the narrow path sound more attractive. In meditation we are turning towards the ever flowing spring of joy that is our own spirit and nothing can ever make this joy sad. It is the life of all things. Diadochos says that we have to desire this with all our energy. Perhaps desire is not the right word. We have to *know* that we need it, we have to know that we already have it and then union happens and the energy of union is joy.

Friendship

St Augustine said that God became human so that we could learn from a human being how we can become divine. The meaning of life is in that deeply Christian insight and meditation makes this meaning come alive in daily life in the experience of profound friendship.

Most people would say that they see the fruits of meditation most of all in their relationships. Firstly, this may mean a more gentle, loving self-acceptance. So often our lives are wrecked, not by others, but by the enemy within, by our own self-rejection or self-hatred. These dark shadows of the psyche are gradually dispelled through meditation because we experience the goodness, we see the loveableness at the core of our being. This doesn't mean that we ignore our faults and failings but we don't see them anymore as essential to ourselves.

In other words, we learn to be friends with ourselves, happier to spend time alone perhaps and to accept that we are a changing mixture of good and bad.

As soon as we become better friends with ourselves we will experience a change in our relationships with other people. Our good relationships may deepen as we learn to pay attention better, to listen and to really care about what other people are feeling. Often the people you live with will be the first to let you know that you are easier to live with.

But most of us have also got problematical relationships as well, people who have hurt or betrayed us in one way or another. Our pain and anger in these relationships can be huge obstacles to our happiness, to our peace, to the simple enjoyment of life and to our spiritual growth. Meditation helps first of all to see and accept these hurt or angry parts of ourselves and gradually they are brought under the influence of the warm, light radiation of the love that is being released in the depth of our being. And never forget that this way of meditation, this way of attention, this way of discipline is above all a way of love.

Don't expect overnight miracles but be open to a surprising liberation from feelings and fears that may have blocked you for many years. Those you think of as your enemies may not suddenly become your favourite people, but you will learn the meaning of forgiveness. To forgive doesn't mean to forget or deny anything. Forgiveness begins with a healing of the wounds within ourselves and if we become deeply friends with every aspect of ourselves we will understand what it means to love your enemies. That truth is freedom and to live in that freedom of love is the Kingdom of God.

So we can see meditation itself as a way of friendship with ourselves and with others. Even strangers appear as peaceful people, more as a potential friend than as a threat or a potential enemy. The experience of this friendship opens us up to the mystery of God, who is the friend of all.

Jesus called his disciples not servants, but friends because he shared with them everything he learned and gained from the friendship he had with God. As you meditate, day by day, you will discover how large this web of friendship is. The very path you are following, your daily meditation, will become a gift of that friendship and the mantra itself as it gently roots itself in your heart, morning and evening, will become a very present and faithful friend.

As you go about your life, responding to challenges, dealing with pain, celebrating joy, the mantra will be there, a link to that deep centre of yourself where you are friends with all creation and all creation is friends with you, because there in your heart you are one with the God who is all, in all.